THE FUNDAMENTALS TOWARD HOMEOWNERSHIP IN FIVE BASIC MISSIONS

An organized planning approach to owning a home using specialized knowledge.

By
John D. Sanabria

Contents

Acknowledgments...pg 4

Preface...pg 5

Introduction... pg 7

Mission #1   *Financing...pg 10*

Mission #2   *Home Search...pg 16*

Mission #3   *Escrow-Title Company... pg 22*

Mission #4   *Insurance... pg 26*

Mission # 5   *The Closing... pg 28*

Helpful links... pg 32

Do's and don'ts... pg 33

About the author... pg 34

Acknowledgements

I would like to thank my amazing wife Marilyn Sanchez for her unwavering support, my sons Brandon and Alexander Sanabria for their input and support and for being my number one fans. Love you guys.

Preface

Thank you for purchasing this book. It has been an exciting journey launching this project, and it is my sincere desire that you gain knowledge from the information presented. In writing this book, my concept has been to keep it as simple as possible. By creating an eagerness to learn more about the home buying process, you will begin your own search for your home. I am sure you have heard "knowledge is power" right? So, the more you learn about buying a home, the better prepared you will be.

My chief aim is to break down the process of purchasing a home in the simplest form possible with techniques that I have personally used many times. This approach, along with the readiness to make your most important purchase, has helped many achieve homeownership. You should feel empowered with this information as you gain direction in devising a plan to work towards your goals of homeownership. The back cover will offer you my motivating factor and vision for this project.

Introduction

There are five fundamentals in which you must have some knowledge, as well as, knowing how to use the *Specialized Knowledge* of others to accomplish your mission to buy-a home.

1. Financing
2. Home Search
3. Title Commitment
4. Home Insurance
5. The Closing

Understanding these fundamentals will imbue you with the confidence needed to make decisions that are in your best interest. Remember, *this is your home*, and all decisions are ultimately yours. It is highly recommended that you make a well-researched decision based on these five basic principles. There are many resources available to help you purchase your new home.

However, understanding the fundamentals in an organized, planned approach by using *specialized knowledge* is the goal of this booklet.

Perhaps, you have heard of these fundamentals in the past. However, my goal is to keep you on task of completing your mission to own a home that results in a favorable outcome with the terms and conditions set to your personal needs. There are many variables to these fundamentals that vary by its respective industry.

In my experience, these missions have a smoother transition when followed in an organized sequential manner.

Let's begin with Your Five Missions.

Financing

Your first mission, perhaps the foundation of homeownership, is how to buy your home if you do not have the capital to pay cash; you finance it. There are many loan programs available to purchase a home. Just Google *Home Loans* and see what happens!

So where do you start? The first step is to review your current personal finances. Under normal circumstances, it is your income verified by your last tax return, your credit report, assets, and reserves that are specific areas you will need to review.

Once you have reviewed your personal finances, take the time to explore the types of home loans available online. At first, you may feel overwhelmed by all the offerings. By seeking the *specialized knowledge* of a professional mortgage lender, you can choose the right loan program for you.

You should contact a minimum of three mortgage lenders. Vetting your lenders is extremely important. Ask questions specific to your needs as you gather mortgage information at this point.

These are examples of questions that should be asked.

How long have you been originating home mortgages with your company?

Experience is good and stability a plus. Lenders that have tenure with their companies tend to be current with changes in the industry as well as being knowledgeable with their underwriting and appraisal staff and timelines.

When are the best times to communicate with you?

Many lending institutions are closed weekends. However, viewing homes and attending open houses. The possibility of having a lender you can communicate during the weekend is always a plus.

Do you offer any niche products?

For several years, I held a position as a Community Reinvestment Mortgage Banking Officer. This is where I learned and originated CRA loans, a niche product.

By asking this question, the lender may be able to have a specialized program that will offer terms more favorable to your financial needs.

Your takeaway by vetting theses lenders is that you are gaining information about their products and services. Most important is the lender's Good Faith Estimate. This item is a listing of all fees you are expected to pay at the time of the closing.

Note: Pay close attention to this document. This is just an estimate and these amounts can be adjusted before closing. and remember it's just an estimate. You will see this document again with final numbers at closing.

Once you have vetted at least three lenders and feel comfortable enough to disclose your personal information, you are now ready to apply for your mortgage. When applying for a home loan, your ultimate goal is to have in hand what is called a "Conditional Loan Approval."

This means that your loan has been through several underwriting steps to ensure you have met their guidelines up to this point. Many professional in the industry call this a "Credit Approved." This is the document you'll need to provide when writing a purchase contract for a home you found to make the offer.

At a minimum, be prepared to provide the following information when applying:

- Two years' worth of W-2 forms on all borrowers
- One month of payroll stubs
- Two months of bank statements for evidence of deposit and closing costs
- Self-employed – two years of federal tax returns with all schedules

- Name, address, and account numbers for all deposit accounts and loans
- If applicable – divorce decree
- Name and address of landlord if renting
- Verification of support payments (income and expense)

Let's move on to your next mission!!

Home Search

Once you have a conditional loan approval in hand, it is time for your next mission of finding your home. This aspect is critical, and it requires a person who has - *specialized knowledge in Real Estate*. At this point, you should seek the assistance of a licensed Realtor ®.

Typically, the assistance of a realtor is free of charge for the buyer, because the seller will pay both buyer and seller agents a commission for their services. (Always confirm this with your agent, as compensation/incentives may differ by state).

Licensed Realtors® have the knowledge, the tools and the up-to-date information in their industry to help you. Realtors are an extremely important component in the process of buying a home. Just as you did with the "Financial Mission," you'll need to do the same with a Realtor® by vetting them. Choosing the right realtor is important.

Sometimes, it may be best not to work with a friend because situations may arise that will cause the buyer to question to integrity of a friend. Unless your realtor has a proven record in real estate, it is necessary to only work with a professional.

Sample questions:

Are you a fulltime agent?
Having an agent that is current and actively engaged in his or her profession is extremely valuable.

How long have you been selling homes "within your targeted area"?

Many agents target areas known as "farm areas. So, if you decide on looking in a completely different area, seeking a realtor that specializes in that new area is highly advisable.

Do you specialize in any specific area of real estate?

Real Estate is a diverse industry; seek a realtor that specializes in Residential Real Estate. A first-time homebuyer, should seek the additional specialized knowledge of a Certified Residential Specialist CRS.

Realtors are a great resource for information that can provide advice, recommendations and support throughout the process of home searches, contract negotiations, home inspections, etc.

Once you have selected a Realtor® it's time for the exciting mission of finding a home. When meeting with a Realtor, share your needs and wants for your new home.

Typically, you should provide: the number of bedrooms and bathrooms, a home with or without a pool, preference for a one- or two-story home, and even specific school districts, etc. If you choose *not to* work with a Real Estate Professional, it is imperative to - have an attorney review any contractual or legal documents. After completing your search with your realtor, you will need to make an offer on the home you have chosen. You should rely on your realtor's specialized knowledge, with the realtor's guidance will assist you with the initial offer.

Your Realtor®, in conjunction with you, will prepare and negotiate the contract as necessary. When negotiating a contract, it is necessary to consider the following before making an offer.

- *How long has the home been on the market and its current condition?*

- *What's the current market like? Is it a buyer's market or seller's market?*

- *Are there any other offers on the property?*

- *Comparable sold properties in the neighborhood*

The best way to make an acceptable offer is to compare your offer with a Comparative Market Analysis for the property. Your realtor has access to statistics to help you. This analysis is an examination of the prices at which similar properties in the same area recently sold. It will include vital market information as well as a current market value.

After the offer price as been determined, the terms and conditions have been identified; the Realtor will prepare the contract, present it to the selling agent. In many cases, your realtor will work with you as there may be a need   to negotiate the offer.

When you have a fully executed-accepted contract, you are now ready to open escrow. This is a good time to start gathering information on the utility, cable, moving, and storage companies near your new home. Ask your Realtor for assistance.

Escrow-Title Company

You now have successfully obtained a conditional loan approval and are in possession of a fully executed sales contract. Your next mission is to seek the ***specialized knowledge*** of a professional title company.

What does a title company do? Their role is to make sure that the title to a piece of real estate is legitimate and then issues title insurance for that property. Title insurance protects the lender and/or owner against lawsuits or claims against the property that result from disputes over the title. Title companies also often maintain escrow accounts, that contain the funds needed to close on the home, ensure that this money is used only for settlement and closing costs.

Finally, the title company will ensure that the new titles, deeds, and other documents are filed with the appropriate entities.

Normally the Earnest Money that accompanies the sales contract is delivered to the title company. I recommend you deliver the earnest money personally since the escrow agent wasn't vetted as they are a non interested party to the transaction. I would always ensure that delivering down payments and or earnest money is done in person. You don't want to be victims of predatory practices when wiring money. Let any wiring of funds be conducted between the Title Company and lenders.

Your Realtor is a good source for title companies and could Open Escrow for you; however, since the escrow agent wasn't vetted since they are a non-interested third party in the transaction, its best to meet in person.

This is what I call attaching you to the transaction. You may have to visit or communicate with this office several times as well as on the day you are scheduled to sign your closing documents.

You should buy an owner's title insurance policy that has as little exclusion as possible, and that it covers the full purchase price of the home.

You should feel free to contact the title

company at any time to get answers to your questions on title searches, title abstracts, title insurance, escrow accounts, or closings dates and time.

Insurance

Once you have an accepted contract, a conditional loan approval, and have opened escrow, it is time for your fourth mission of obtaining homeowners insurance.
A licensed homeowner's insurance agent has another area of *specialized knowledge* you will need to leverage.

Homeowner insurance is a specific type of insurance policy that protects the homeowners against losses and damage caused by perils, such as fires, storms, or burglary. It also covers legal costs if someone is injured in your home or on your property. Earthquake and flood coverage are typically not included in standard homeowner's insurance policies, but you may be able to add on this additional coverage. (Note: flood insurance is often required in flood zones.) Your home insurance premium is typically paid monthly, along with your mortgage payment, mortgage insurance premiums, and taxes can be set up with your lender. This is also known as "Impounding."

    Homeowners insurance is almost always required to get a home loan. Remember your homeowner's insurance will impact your total mortgage payment.

The Closing

Your fifth and final mission is the exchange of the property from the seller to you as the buyer. The money, deed and its transfer, and final loan paperwork are part of the legal transfer of ownership to you. Most Realtors, along with the buyers, will do a and a walk through of the property. The closing occurs when all conditions of the contract have been met. There must be a full loan approval, evidence of clear title, homeowner's insurance, and mortgage insurance when required. Prior to the actual closing date, both the buyer and the seller can expect to review the list of fees and the terms and conditions of the contract. In addition, you will be informed of the exact amount of money needed to complete the transaction. Your real estate agent, lender, and the title company will assist you with this process. Normally, a cashier's check is required.

The lender arranges the closing and ensures that the closing agent has all the necessary documents in place. The closing may take place at a closing attorney's office or at a title or escrow company. At the closing, the lender "funds" the loan with a cashier's check, draft, or wire to the closing agent who disburses funds in exchange for the title to the property.

This is the point at which transfer of ownership occurs and the buyer receives possession of the property. With any legal transactions, there will be many forms to sign. It is necessity that you should carefully review all documents before signing. Do not hesitate to ask questions to address your concerns. The closing agent can explain everything to you.

Congratulations!

You have successfully completed all five missions.

Moving day into your new home has arrived.

Recommended actions to take

- *Contact - a locksmith to rekey your home.*

- *Purchase a fireproof safe for the important documents issued at closing.*

- *Install a home security system*

Helpful Links:

Mortgage Calculator:

http://www.mortgagecalculator.org

National Association of Realtors:

http://www.realtor.org

National Association of Mortgage Bankers:

http://www.namb.org

The American Land Title Association:

http://www.alta.org

Credit Reporting Agencies:

Trans-Union:

www.transunion.com

Experian:

www.experian.com

Equifax:

www.equifax.com

Do's and Don'ts

Do's

- *Order and Review your credit prior to applying for a home loan. Most of them are free now, and it might not impact your score.*
- *Gather all financial information such as 401k, savings account, stocks, bonds etc.*
- *Save, save and save your money.*

Don'ts

- *Do not buy anything on credit while in the process of buying a home*
- *Do not change jobs unless it is for more money be advised that your closing will be delayed by a minimum of four weeks*
- *Do not deposit large amounts of money into any accounts you have disclosed to your lender prior to their approval because this could be considered a gifts that will need to be documented.*

About the Author

John D. Sanabria has been in the housing industry for over twenty-four years. His career in the housing industry began as a Mortgage Originator in Arizona shortly after returning from Desert Storm. Seven years later, he obtained his Real Estate® licence.

His experience derives from being part of some of the largest companies and amazing leaders in their industry. He has had the privilege of assisting both buyers and sellers achieve their goals of homeownership with a full range of real estate services by empowering his clients with information, guidance, and a clear path to a successful real estate experience.

For additional information and ordering, contact:

John D. Sanabria

Phone: (407) 552-7582

Email:

jsanabria747@hotmail.com

Back cover photo provided
by
Kenzie Head

Your support of the author's rights is appreciated.

September 13, 2016   DATE   V. 1.2

Notes:

www.ingramcontent.com/pod-product-compliance
Lightning Source LLC
Chambersburg PA
CBHW031558210526
45464CB00003B/1327